Stop Now
Enjoy The Moment
It's Now Or Never

According to Harvard Medical School, gratitude is:

"a thankful appreciation for what an individual receives,
whether tangible or intangible.
With gratitude, people acknowledge the goodness in their lives.
As a result, gratitude also helps people connect to something larger
than themselves as individuals – whether to other people,
nature, or a higher power"

"The more grateful I am, the more beauty I see." / Mary Davis /

I AM GRATEFUL FOR THESE SIMPLE THINGS

I AM GRATEFUL FOR THESE PEOPLE

DAILY REFLECTION

I AM GRATEFUL FOR
THESE SIMPLE THINGS

I AM GRATEFUL FOR
THESE PEOPLE

DAILY REFLECTION

Enjoy Every Moment

I AM GRATEFUL FOR THESE SIMPLE THINGS

I AM GRATEFUL FOR THESE PEOPLE

DAILY REFLECTION

TODAY IS

_____ / _____ / _____

I AM GRATEFUL FOR
THESE SIMPLE THINGS

I AM GRATEFUL FOR
THESE PEOPLE

DAILY REFLECTION

"Start each day with a positive thought and a grateful heart."
/ Ray T. Bennett /

I AM GRATEFUL FOR THESE SIMPLE THINGS

I AM GRATEFUL FOR THESE PEOPLE

DAILY REFLECTION

I AM GRATEFUL FOR
THESE SIMPLE THINGS

I AM GRATEFUL FOR
THESE PEOPLE

DAILY REFLECTION

"True forgiveness is when you can say, "Thank you for that experience."
/ Oprah Winfrey /

I AM GRATEFUL FOR THESE SIMPLE THINGS

I AM GRATEFUL FOR THESE PEOPLE

DAILY REFLECTION

TODAY IS

.... / .... / ....

I AM GRATEFUL FOR
THESE SIMPLE THINGS

I AM GRATEFUL FOR
THESE PEOPLE

DAILY REFLECTION

Gratitude is the Best Attitude

I AM GRATEFUL FOR THESE SIMPLE THINGS

I AM GRATEFUL FOR THESE PEOPLE

DAILY REFLECTION

................../................../..................

I AM GRATEFUL FOR
THESE SIMPLE THINGS

I AM GRATEFUL FOR
THESE PEOPLE

DAILY REFLECTION

"Great things happen to those who don't stop believing, trying, learning, and being grateful" / Roy T. Bennett /

I AM GRATEFUL FOR THESE SIMPLE THINGS

I AM GRATEFUL FOR THESE PEOPLE

DAILY REFLECTION

I AM GRATEFUL FOR THESE SIMPLE THINGS

I AM GRATEFUL FOR THESE PEOPLE

DAILY REFLECTION

"At the end of the day, let there be no excuses, no explanations, no regrets." / Steve Maraboli /

I AM GRATEFUL FOR THESE SIMPLE THINGS

I AM GRATEFUL FOR THESE PEOPLE

DAILY REFLECTION

I AM GRATEFUL FOR
THESE SIMPLE THINGS

I AM GRATEFUL FOR
THESE PEOPLE

DAILY REFLECTION

"We must find time to stop and thank the people
who make a difference in our lives" / John F. Kennedy /

I AM GRATEFUL FOR THESE SIMPLE THINGS

I AM GRATEFUL FOR THESE PEOPLE

DAILY REFLECTION

I AM GRATEFUL FOR
THESE SIMPLE THINGS

I AM GRATEFUL FOR
THESE PEOPLE

DAILY REFLECTION

"When we give cheerfully and accept gratefully, everyone is blessed" / Maya Angelou /

I AM GRATEFUL FOR THESE SIMPLE THINGS

I AM GRATEFUL FOR THESE PEOPLE

DAILY REFLECTION

I AM GRATEFUL FOR
THESE SIMPLE THINGS

I AM GRATEFUL FOR
THESE PEOPLE

DAILY REFLECTION

"Joy is the simplest form of gratitude."
/ Karl Barth /

I AM GRATEFUL FOR
THESE SIMPLE THINGS

I AM GRATEFUL FOR
THESE PEOPLE

DAILY REFLECTION

I AM GRATEFUL FOR THESE SIMPLE THINGS

I AM GRATEFUL FOR THESE PEOPLE

DAILY REFLECTION

"No one who achieves success does so without the help of others.
The wise and confident acknowledge this help with gratitude."
/ Alfred North Whitehead /

I AM GRATEFUL FOR
THESE SIMPLE THINGS

I AM GRATEFUL FOR
THESE PEOPLE

DAILY REFLECTION

TODAY IS

.... / /

I AM GRATEFUL FOR
THESE SIMPLE THINGS

I AM GRATEFUL FOR
THESE PEOPLE

DAILY REFLECTION

"In ordinary life, we hardly realize that we receive
a great deal more than we give, and that it is only
with gratitude that life becomes rich" / Dietrich Bonhoeffer /

TODAY IS
/ /

I AM GRATEFUL FOR
THESE SIMPLE THINGS

I AM GRATEFUL FOR
THESE PEOPLE

DAILY REFLECTION

TODAY IS

.............../........../...............

I AM GRATEFUL FOR
THESE SIMPLE THINGS

I AM GRATEFUL FOR
THESE PEOPLE

DAILY REFLECTION

"My expectations were reduced to zero when I was 21. Everything since then has been a bonus." / Stephen W. Hawking /

I AM GRATEFUL FOR THESE SIMPLE THINGS

I AM GRATEFUL FOR THESE PEOPLE

DAILY REFLECTION

I AM GRATEFUL FOR
THESE SIMPLE THINGS

I AM GRATEFUL FOR
THESE PEOPLE

DAILY REFLECTION

"Gratitude is not only the greatest of virtues but the parent of all others." / Marcus Tullius Cicero /

I AM GRATEFUL FOR THESE SIMPLE THINGS

I AM GRATEFUL FOR THESE PEOPLE

DAILY REFLECTION

I AM GRATEFUL FOR
THESE SIMPLE THINGS

I AM GRATEFUL FOR
THESE PEOPLE

DAILY REFLECTION

"Appreciation is a wonderful thing. It makes what is excellent in others belong to us as well." / Voltaire /

I AM GRATEFUL FOR THESE SIMPLE THINGS

I AM GRATEFUL FOR THESE PEOPLE

DAILY REFLECTION

/ /

I AM GRATEFUL FOR
THESE SIMPLE THINGS

I AM GRATEFUL FOR
THESE PEOPLE

DAILY REFLECTION

"You cannot do a kindness too soon because
you never know how soon it will be too late." / Ralph Waldo Emerson /

I AM GRATEFUL FOR
THESE SIMPLE THINGS

I AM GRATEFUL FOR
THESE PEOPLE

DAILY REFLECTION

/ /

I AM GRATEFUL FOR
THESE SIMPLE THINGS

I AM GRATEFUL FOR
THESE PEOPLE

DAILY REFLECTION

"The highest tribute to the dead is not grief but gratitude."
/ Thornton Wilder /

I AM GRATEFUL FOR THESE SIMPLE THINGS

I AM GRATEFUL FOR THESE PEOPLE

DAILY REFLECTION

.... / .... /

I AM GRATEFUL FOR
THESE SIMPLE THINGS

I AM GRATEFUL FOR
THESE PEOPLE

DAILY REFLECTION

"Gratitude will shift you to a higher frequency, and you will attract much better things." / Rhonda Byrne /

I AM GRATEFUL FOR THESE SIMPLE THINGS

I AM GRATEFUL FOR THESE PEOPLE

DAILY REFLECTION

I AM GRATEFUL FOR
THESE SIMPLE THINGS

I AM GRATEFUL FOR
THESE PEOPLE

DAILY REFLECTION

"When I started counting my blessings, my whole life turned around" / Willie Nelson /

I AM GRATEFUL FOR THESE SIMPLE THINGS

I AM GRATEFUL FOR THESE PEOPLE

DAILY REFLECTION

TODAY IS

.... / /

I AM GRATEFUL FOR
THESE SIMPLE THINGS

I AM GRATEFUL FOR
THESE PEOPLE

DAILY REFLECTION

"Gratitude helps you to grow and expand; gratitude brings joy and laughter into your life and into the lives of all those around you." / Eileen Caddy /

I AM GRATEFUL FOR THESE SIMPLE THINGS

I AM GRATEFUL FOR THESE PEOPLE

DAILY REFLECTION

TODAY IS

/ /

I AM GRATEFUL FOR
THESE SIMPLE THINGS

I AM GRATEFUL FOR
THESE PEOPLE

DAILY REFLECTION

"Two kinds of gratitude: The sudden kind
we feel for what we take; the larger kind
we feel for what we give." / Edwin Arlington Robinson /

I AM GRATEFUL FOR THESE SIMPLE THINGS

I AM GRATEFUL FOR THESE PEOPLE

DAILY REFLECTION

TODAY IS

_____ / _____ / _____

I AM GRATEFUL FOR
THESE SIMPLE THINGS

I AM GRATEFUL FOR
THESE PEOPLE

DAILY REFLECTION

"Gratitude is the sweetest thing in a seekers life - in all human life.
If there is gratitude in your heart, then there will be tremendous sweetness in your eyes."
/ Sri Chinmoy /

I AM GRATEFUL FOR THESE SIMPLE THINGS

I AM GRATEFUL FOR THESE PEOPLE

DAILY REFLECTION

I AM GRATEFUL FOR
THESE SIMPLE THINGS

I AM GRATEFUL FOR
THESE PEOPLE

DAILY REFLECTION

"The more grateful I am, the more beauty I see."
/ Mary Davis /

I AM GRATEFUL FOR
THESE SIMPLE THINGS

I AM GRATEFUL FOR
THESE PEOPLE

DAILY REFLECTION

I AM GRATEFUL FOR
THESE SIMPLE THINGS

I AM GRATEFUL FOR
THESE PEOPLE

DAILY REFLECTION

"The deepest craving of human nature
is the need to be appreciated" / William James /

I AM GRATEFUL FOR
THESE SIMPLE THINGS

I AM GRATEFUL FOR
THESE PEOPLE

DAILY REFLECTION

I AM GRATEFUL FOR
THESE SIMPLE THINGS

I AM GRATEFUL FOR
THESE PEOPLE

DAILY REFLECTION

"There is a calmness to a life lived in gratitude, a quiet joy." / Ralph H. Blum /

I AM GRATEFUL FOR
THESE SIMPLE THINGS

I AM GRATEFUL FOR
THESE PEOPLE

DAILY REFLECTION

TODAY IS

_____ / _____ / _____

I AM GRATEFUL FOR
THESE SIMPLE THINGS
_____

I AM GRATEFUL FOR
THESE PEOPLE
_____

_____

_____

_____

_____

_____

_____

_____

_____

_____

DAILY REFLECTION
_____

"Gratitude is the most exquisite form of courtesy."
/ Jacques Maritain /

I AM GRATEFUL FOR
THESE SIMPLE THINGS

I AM GRATEFUL FOR
THESE PEOPLE

DAILY REFLECTION

I AM GRATEFUL FOR
THESE SIMPLE THINGS

I AM GRATEFUL FOR
THESE PEOPLE

DAILY REFLECTION

"The root of joy is gratefulness." / David Steindl-Rast /

I AM GRATEFUL FOR THESE SIMPLE THINGS

I AM GRATEFUL FOR THESE PEOPLE

DAILY REFLECTION

I AM GRATEFUL FOR
THESE SIMPLE THINGS

I AM GRATEFUL FOR
THESE PEOPLE

DAILY REFLECTION

"He is a wise man who does not grieve for the things which he has not, but rejoices for those which he has." / Epictetus /

TODAY IS

_____ / /

I AM GRATEFUL FOR THESE SIMPLE THINGS

I AM GRATEFUL FOR THESE PEOPLE

DAILY REFLECTION

I AM GRATEFUL FOR
THESE SIMPLE THINGS

I AM GRATEFUL FOR
THESE PEOPLE

DAILY REFLECTION

"Being thankful is not always experienced as a natural state of existence, we must work at it, akin to a type of trength training for the heart." / Larissa Gomez /

I AM GRATEFUL FOR THESE SIMPLE THINGS

I AM GRATEFUL FOR THESE PEOPLE

DAILY REFLECTION

I AM GRATEFUL FOR
THESE SIMPLE THINGS

I AM GRATEFUL FOR
THESE PEOPLE

DAILY REFLECTION

"We can only be said to be alive in those moments when our hearts are conscious of our treasures." / Thornton Wilder /

I AM GRATEFUL FOR THESE SIMPLE THINGS

I AM GRATEFUL FOR THESE PEOPLE

DAILY REFLECTION

TODAY IS

.... / .... /

I AM GRATEFUL FOR
THESE SIMPLE THINGS

I AM GRATEFUL FOR
THESE PEOPLE

DAILY REFLECTION

"Be thankful for what you have; you'll end up having more.
If you concentrate on what you don't have, you will never, ever have enough"
/ Oprah Winfrey /

I AM GRATEFUL FOR
THESE SIMPLE THINGS

I AM GRATEFUL FOR
THESE PEOPLE

DAILY REFLECTION

I AM GRATEFUL FOR
THESE SIMPLE THINGS

I AM GRATEFUL FOR
THESE PEOPLE

DAILY REFLECTION

"As we express our gratitude, we must never forget
that the highest appreciation is not to utter words, but to live by them"
/ John F. Kennedy /

I AM GRATEFUL FOR
THESE SIMPLE THINGS

I AM GRATEFUL FOR
THESE PEOPLE

DAILY REFLECTION

I AM GRATEFUL FOR
THESE SIMPLE THINGS

I AM GRATEFUL FOR
THESE PEOPLE

DAILY REFLECTION

"Gratitude for the present moment and the fullness of life now is the true prosperity." / Eckhart Tolle /

I AM GRATEFUL FOR THESE SIMPLE THINGS

I AM GRATEFUL FOR THESE PEOPLE

_____

_____

_____

_____

_____

_____

_____

_____

_____

_____

DAILY REFLECTION

TODAY IS

.... / .... / ....

I AM GRATEFUL FOR
THESE SIMPLE THINGS

I AM GRATEFUL FOR
THESE PEOPLE

DAILY REFLECTION

"Gratitude is the sign of noble souls."
/ Aesop /

I AM GRATEFUL FOR THESE SIMPLE THINGS

I AM GRATEFUL FOR THESE PEOPLE

DAILY REFLECTION

I AM GRATEFUL FOR
THESE SIMPLE THINGS

I AM GRATEFUL FOR
THESE PEOPLE

DAILY REFLECTION

"Feeling gratitude and not expressing it is like wrapping a present and not giving it." / William Arthur Ward /

I AM GRATEFUL FOR THESE SIMPLE THINGS

I AM GRATEFUL FOR THESE PEOPLE

DAILY REFLECTION

/ /

I AM GRATEFUL FOR
THESE SIMPLE THINGS

I AM GRATEFUL FOR
THESE PEOPLE

DAILY REFLECTION

"Opening your eyes to more of the world around you can deeply enhance your gratitude practice." / Derrick Carpenter /

I AM GRATEFUL FOR THESE SIMPLE THINGS

I AM GRATEFUL FOR THESE PEOPLE

DAILY REFLECTION

I AM GRATEFUL FOR
THESE SIMPLE THINGS

I AM GRATEFUL FOR
THESE PEOPLE

DAILY REFLECTION

"Nothing is more honorable than a grateful heart."
/ Lucius Annaeus Seneca /

TODAY IS

___ / ___ / ___

I AM GRATEFUL FOR THESE SIMPLE THINGS

I AM GRATEFUL FOR THESE PEOPLE

DAILY REFLECTION

........./......./............

I AM GRATEFUL FOR
THESE SIMPLE THINGS

I AM GRATEFUL FOR
THESE PEOPLE

DAILY REFLECTION

"Train yourself never to put off the word or action for the expression of gratitude." / Albert Schweitzer /

I AM GRATEFUL FOR THESE SIMPLE THINGS

I AM GRATEFUL FOR THESE PEOPLE

DAILY REFLECTION

········· / /

I AM GRATEFUL FOR
THESE SIMPLE THINGS

I AM GRATEFUL FOR
THESE PEOPLE

DAILY REFLECTION

"Gratitude is riches. Complaint is poverty." / Doris Day /

I AM GRATEFUL FOR THESE SIMPLE THINGS

I AM GRATEFUL FOR THESE PEOPLE

DAILY REFLECTION

TODAY IS

............./......../............

I AM GRATEFUL FOR
THESE SIMPLE THINGS

I AM GRATEFUL FOR
THESE PEOPLE

DAILY REFLECTION

"When you are grateful, fear disappears and abundance appears." / Anthony Robbins /

TODAY IS

.............../ / /

I AM GRATEFUL FOR THESE SIMPLE THINGS

I AM GRATEFUL FOR THESE PEOPLE

DAILY REFLECTION

I AM GRATEFUL FOR
THESE SIMPLE THINGS

I AM GRATEFUL FOR
THESE PEOPLE

DAILY REFLECTION

"What separates privilege from entitlement is gratitude."
/ Brene Brown /

I AM GRATEFUL FOR THESE SIMPLE THINGS

I AM GRATEFUL FOR THESE PEOPLE

DAILY REFLECTION

TODAY IS

_____ / _____ / _____

I AM GRATEFUL FOR
THESE SIMPLE THINGS

I AM GRATEFUL FOR
THESE PEOPLE

_____

_____

_____

_____

_____

_____

_____

_____

_____

DAILY REFLECTION

/ /

"When it comes to life the critical thing is whether you take things for granted or take them with gratitude." / G.K. Chesterton /

I AM GRATEFUL FOR THESE SIMPLE THINGS

I AM GRATEFUL FOR THESE PEOPLE

DAILY REFLECTION

I AM GRATEFUL FOR
THESE SIMPLE THINGS

I AM GRATEFUL FOR
THESE PEOPLE

DAILY REFLECTION

"Gratitude makes sense of our past,
brings peace for today, and creates a vision for tomorrow." / Melody Beattie /

I AM GRATEFUL FOR
THESE SIMPLE THINGS

I AM GRATEFUL FOR
THESE PEOPLE

DAILY REFLECTION

TODAY IS

.... / / ....

I AM GRATEFUL FOR
THESE SIMPLE THINGS

I AM GRATEFUL FOR
THESE PEOPLE

DAILY REFLECTION

"Gratitude turns what we have into enough." / Anonymous /

I AM GRATEFUL FOR THESE SIMPLE THINGS

I AM GRATEFUL FOR THESE PEOPLE

DAILY REFLECTION

I AM GRATEFUL FOR
THESE SIMPLE THINGS

I AM GRATEFUL FOR
THESE PEOPLE

DAILY REFLECTION

"Gratitude is the fairest blossom
which springs from the soul" / Henry Ward Beecher /

I AM GRATEFUL FOR THESE SIMPLE THINGS

I AM GRATEFUL FOR THESE PEOPLE

DAILY REFLECTION

I AM GRATEFUL FOR
THESE SIMPLE THINGS

I AM GRATEFUL FOR
THESE PEOPLE

DAILY REFLECTION

"Gratitude is a powerful catalyst for happiness.
It's the spark that lights a fire of joy in your soul" / Amy Collette /

I AM GRATEFUL FOR
THESE SIMPLE THINGS

I AM GRATEFUL FOR
THESE PEOPLE

_____

_____

_____

_____

_____

_____

_____

_____

_____

_____

DAILY REFLECTION

TODAY IS

.... / .... / ....

I AM GRATEFUL FOR
THESE SIMPLE THINGS

I AM GRATEFUL FOR
THESE PEOPLE

DAILY REFLECTION

"If the only prayer you said was thank you, that would be enough." / Meister Eckhart /

I AM GRATEFUL FOR
THESE SIMPLE THINGS

I AM GRATEFUL FOR
THESE PEOPLE

DAILY REFLECTION

TODAY IS

_____ / _____ / _____

I AM GRATEFUL FOR
THESE SIMPLE THINGS

I AM GRATEFUL FOR
THESE PEOPLE

DAILY REFLECTION

"Thankfulness is the beginning of gratitude. Gratitude is the completion of thankfulness. Thankfulness may consist merely of words. Gratitude is shown in acts." / Henri Frederic Amiel /

I AM GRATEFUL FOR THESE SIMPLE THINGS

I AM GRATEFUL FOR THESE PEOPLE

DAILY REFLECTION

TODAY IS
........................./......./

I AM GRATEFUL FOR
THESE SIMPLE THINGS

I AM GRATEFUL FOR
THESE PEOPLE

DAILY REFLECTION

"Happiness cannot be traveled to owned,
earned, worn or consumed Happiness is the spiritual
experience of living every minute with love, grace, and gratitude." / Denis Waitley /

I AM GRATEFUL FOR
THESE SIMPLE THINGS

I AM GRATEFUL FOR
THESE PEOPLE

DAILY REFLECTION

TODAY IS

_____ / _____ / _____

I AM GRATEFUL FOR
THESE SIMPLE THINGS
_____

I AM GRATEFUL FOR
THESE PEOPLE
_____

_____

_____

_____

_____

_____

_____

_____

_____

_____

DAILY REFLECTION
_____

"We often take for granted the very things that most deserve our gratitude." / Cynthia Ozick /

I AM GRATEFUL FOR THESE SIMPLE THINGS

I AM GRATEFUL FOR THESE PEOPLE

DAILY REFLECTION

I AM GRATEFUL FOR
THESE SIMPLE THINGS

I AM GRATEFUL FOR
THESE PEOPLE

DAILY REFLECTION

"Gratitude is when memory is stored
in the heart and not in the mind" / Lionel Hampton /

I AM GRATEFUL FOR
THESE SIMPLE THINGS

I AM GRATEFUL FOR
THESE PEOPLE

DAILY REFLECTION

I AM GRATEFUL FOR
THESE SIMPLE THINGS

I AM GRATEFUL FOR
THESE PEOPLE

DAILY REFLECTION

"I would maintain that thanks are the highest form of thought, and that gratitude is happiness doubled by wonder."
/ Gilbert C. Chesterton /

I AM GRATEFUL FOR THESE SIMPLE THINGS

I AM GRATEFUL FOR THESE PEOPLE

DAILY REFLECTION

I AM GRATEFUL FOR
THESE SIMPLE THINGS

I AM GRATEFUL FOR
THESE PEOPLE

DAILY REFLECTION

"Never in the field of human conflict was so much owed by so many to so few." / Winston Churchill /

I AM GRATEFUL FOR
THESE SIMPLE THINGS

I AM GRATEFUL FOR
THESE PEOPLE

DAILY REFLECTION

I AM GRATEFUL FOR
THESE SIMPLE THINGS

I AM GRATEFUL FOR
THESE PEOPLE

DAILY REFLECTION

"Breath is the finest gift of nature.
Be grateful for this wonderful gift." / Amit Ray /

I AM GRATEFUL FOR
THESE SIMPLE THINGS

I AM GRATEFUL FOR
THESE PEOPLE

DAILY REFLECTION

TODAY IS

.... / .... / ....

I AM GRATEFUL FOR
THESE SIMPLE THINGS

I AM GRATEFUL FOR
THESE PEOPLE

DAILY REFLECTION

Made in the USA
Monee, IL
08 November 2023

46059981R00063